D0423248

KEEP
CALM
FOR
BRIDES

KEEP CALM FOR BRIDES

Summersdale Publishers Ltd
46 West Street
Chichester
West Sussex
PO19 1RP
UK

www.summersdale.com

Printed and bound in the Czech Republic

ISBN: 978-1-84953-241-9

Substantial discounts on bulk quantities of Summersdale books are available to corporations, professional associations and other organisations. For details telephone Summersdale Publishers on (+44-1243-771107), fax (+44-1243-786300) or email (nicky@summersdale.com).

KEEP
CALM
FOR
BRIDES

summersdale

CONTENTS

MARRIAGE

Happy marriages begin
when we marry the ones
we love, and they blossom
when we love the ones
we marry.

Tom Mullen

Between husband and wife friendship seems to exist by nature, for man is naturally disposed to pairing.

Aristotle

Marriages are made in heaven.

Proverb

Marriage resembles a pair of shears, so joined that they cannot be separated; often moving in opposite directions, yet always punishing anyone who comes between them.

Sydney Smith

To get the full value
of joy you must have
someone to divide
it with.

Mark Twain

One should believe
in marriage as in the
immortality of the soul.

Honoré de Balzac

Marriage is the
perfection of what
love aimed at.

Ralph Waldo Emerson

What counts in making a happy marriage is not so much how compatible you are, but how you deal with incompatibility.

Leo Tolstoy

A good marriage is like a casserole: only those responsible for it really know what goes in it.

Anonymous

Marriage is the golden
ring in a chain whose
beginning is a glance
and whose ending
is eternity.

Khalil Gibran

A married couple are well
suited when both partners
usually feel the need for a
quarrel at the same time.

Jean Rostand

Being married is like having somebody permanently in your corner, it feels limitless, not limited.

Gloria Steinem

We don't take ourselves too seriously, and laughter is the best form of unity, I think, in a marriage.

Michelle Obama

It is not your love that
sustains the marriage, but
from now on, the marriage
that sustains your love.

Dietrich Bonhoeffer

What a happy and holy fashion it is that those who love one another should rest on the same pillow.

Nathaniel Hawthorne

Being married is like having a colour television set. You never want to go back to black and white.

Danny Perosa

What greater thing
is there for two human
souls than to feel that
they are joined
for life...

George Eliot

Love seems the swiftest,
but it is the slowest of all
growths. No man or woman
really knows what perfect
love is until they have been
married a quarter of
a century.

Mark Twain

The bonds of
matrimony are like
any other bonds –
they mature slowly.

Peter De Vries

Marriage is the mother of the world and preserves kingdoms, and fills cities, and churches, and heaven itself.

Jeremy Taylor

The sum which two married
people owe to one another
defies calculation. It is an
infinite debt, which can only
be discharged through
all eternity.

Johann Wolfgang von Goethe,
Elective Affinities

A happy marriage is a new beginning of life, a new starting point for happiness and usefulness.

Arthur Penrhyn Stanley

Marriage should be
a duet – when one
sings, the other claps.

Joe Murray

A successful marriage
requires falling in love
many times, always
with the same person.

Mignon McLaughlin

Chains do not hold a marriage together. It is threads, hundreds of tiny threads, which sew people together through the years.

Simone Signoret

If ever two were one,
then surely we.
If ever man were lov'd
by wife, then thee.

Anne Bradstreet

If I get married, I want
to be very married.

Audrey Hepburn

Marriage is an investment
which pays dividends if you
pay interest.

Bob Monkhouse

When a marriage
works, nothing on
earth can take
its place.

Helen Gahagan

A happy marriage is
a long conversation
which always seems
too short.

André Maurois

For marriage to be a
success, every woman and
every man should have her
and his own bathroom.
The end.

Catherine Zeta-Jones

It's so great to find that one
special person you want to
annoy for the rest of
your life.

Rita Rudner

In my house I'm the boss, my wife is just the decision maker.

Woody Allen

Marriage is not just spiritual communion, it is also remembering to take out the trash.

Dr Joyce Brothers

One doesn't have to get anywhere in a marriage. It's not a public conveyance.

Iris Murdoch

Each moment of a happy lover's hour is worth an age of dull and common life.

Aphra Behn

The heart of marriage
is memories.

Bill Cosby

There is no more lovely,
friendly and charming
relationship, communion
or company than a
good marriage.

Martin Luther

Keep your eyes wide
open before marriage,
half shut afterwards.

Benjamin Franklin

Marriage is our last,
best chance to
grow up.

Joseph Barth

Heaven will be no heaven to me if I do not meet my wife there.

Andrew Jackson

A good marriage is like a good trade: each thinks he got the better deal.

Ivern Ball

The highest happiness
on earth is marriage.

William Lyon Phelps

There is no such cosy
combination as man
and wife.

Menander

No road is long with good company.

Turkish proverb

A smile is the
beginning of peace.

Mother Teresa

BRIDES

A man's wife has more
power over him than
the state has.

Ralph Waldo Emerson

I... chose my wife, as she did her wedding gown, not for a fine glossy surface, but such qualities as would wear well.

Oliver Goldsmith,
The Vicar of Wakefield

If you think women are the
weaker sex, trying pulling
the blankets back to
your side.

Stuart Turner

An ideal wife is any woman who has an ideal husband.

Booth Tarkington

If they like your little jokes before you're married, afterwards they ask why you're always trying to be funny.

J. B. Priestley

It is a truth universally acknowledged, that a single man in possession of a good fortune, must be in want of a wife.

Jane Austen, *Pride and Prejudice*

The most precious
possession that ever comes
to man in this world is a
woman's heart.

J. G. Holland

I haven't spoken to my wife in years – I didn't want to interrupt her.

Rodney Dangerfield

Those who bring
sunshine into the lives
of others cannot keep
it from themselves.

J. M. Barrie

GROOMS

It's true what they say
– all the good men
are married. But it's
marriage that makes
them good.

Gay Talese

When you meet someone
who can cook and do
housework – don't hesitate
a minute – marry him.

Anonymous

When a wife has a
good husband it is
easily seen in
her face.

Johann Wolfgang von Goethe

The man who says his wife
can't take a joke, forgets
that she took him.

Oscar Wilde

May the gods grant you
all things which your heart
desires, and may they give
you a husband and a home
and gracious concord, for
there is nothing greater and
better than this.

Homer

Why can't women tell jokes? Because we marry them!

Kathy Lette

The calmest husbands make the stormiest wives.

English proverb

Men always want to be a woman's first love. That is their clumsy vanity. We women have a more subtle instinct about things. What we like is to be a man's last romance.

Oscar Wilde,
A Woman of No Importance

If a man speaks in the forest, and there's no woman around to hear him, is he still wrong?

Rich Makin

But he that is married careth for the things that are of the world, how he may please his wife.

Bible, Corinthians 7:33

No woman ever shot
her husband while he
was doing the dishes.

George Coote

Don't worry, if you keep him
long enough he'll come
back in style.

Dorothy Parker

How can a woman be expected to be happy with a man who insists on treating her as if she were a perfectly normal human being?

Oscar Wilde

My mom said the only reason men are alive is for lawn care and vehicle maintenance.

Tim Allen

Have patience with
all things, but chiefly
have patience with
yourself.

St Francis de Sales

RELATIONS

Be kind to your mother-in-law, but pay for her board at some good hotel.

Josh Billings

I don't think anyone
has a normal family.

Edward Furlong

The awe and dread with which the untutored savage contemplates his mother-in-law are amongst the most familiar facts of anthropology.

James George Frazer

Humour is always based on a modicum of truth. Have you ever heard a joke about a father-in-law?

Dick Clark

God gives us
relatives; thank God,
we can choose
our friends.

Addison Mizner

Never rely on the glory of
the morning or the smiles of
your mother-in-law.

Japanese proverb

The day my mother-in-law called, the mice threw themselves on the traps.

Les Dawson

Friends are God's
apology for relations.

Hugh Kingsmill

I just got back from a
pleasure trip. Drove my
mother-in-law to the airport.

Rodney Dangerfield

Behind every
successful man
stands a surprised
mother-in-law.

Hubert Humphrey

The pursuit, even of
the best things, ought to
be calm and tranquil.

Cicero

PLANNING

One has to resign
oneself to being a
nuisance if one wants
to get anything done.

Freya Stark

After all there is something about a wedding-gown prettier than in any other gown in the world.

Douglas William Jerrold

It is difficult to see why lace should be so expensive; it is mostly holes.

Mary Wilson Little

The less one has to do the less time one finds to do it.

Anonymous

We experience moments
absolutely free from worry.
These brief respites are
called panic.

Cullen Hightower

Mix a little
foolishness with your
serious plans. It is
lovely to be silly at the
right moment.

Horace

THE
WEDDING

He that hath the bride is the bridegroom: but the friend of the bridegroom, which standeth and heareth him, rejoiceth greatly because of the bridegroom's voice: this my joy therefore is fulfilled.

Bible, John 3:29

Builders, raise the
ceiling high,
Raise the dome into the sky,
Hear the wedding song!
For the happy groom
is near,
Tall as Mars, and statelier,
Hear the wedding song!

Sappho

It's not as great a day for the bride as she thinks. She's not marrying the best man.

Anonymous

There is no greater feeling than when a groom turns to see his bride and has tears in his eyes because she is so beautiful.

Tim Alan

A happy bridesmaid
makes a happy bride.

Alfred Tennyson

A cloudy day
is no match for a
sunny disposition.

William Arthur Ward

THE
RECEPTION

A feast is made for laughter, and wine maketh merry.

Bible, Ecclesiastes 10:19

The art of hospitality is to make guests feel at home when you wish they were.

Violet Smart

Let us celebrate the occasion with wine and sweet words.

Plautus

A gloomy guest fits
not a wedding feast.

Friedrich Schiller

Every guest hates the others, and the host hates them all.

Albanian proverb

Bugger the table plan,
give me my dinner!

Prince Philip
(at a dinner party at Broadlands)

The human brain starts
working the moment you are
born and never stops until
you stand to speak in public.

George Jessel

The trouble with being the best man at a wedding is that you never get to prove it.

Anonymous

In all of the wedding cake, hope is the sweetest of plums.

Douglas William Jerrold

If it were not for the presents, an elopement would be preferable.

George Ade

A well-spent
day brings happy
sleep.

Leonardo da Vinci

LOVE

Love is not looking in each other's eyes, but looking together in the same direction.

Antoine de Saint-Exupéry

Doubt thou the stars are fire;
Doubt that the sun
doth move;
Doubt truth to be a liar;
But never doubt I love you.

William Shakespeare, *Hamlet*

There is only one happiness in life, to love and be loved.

George Sand

Love is but the discovery of
ourselves in others, and the
delight in the recognition.

Alexander Smith

Who, being loved,
is poor?

Oscar Wilde

Love cures people, the ones
who receive love and the
ones who give it, too.

Karl Menninger

Love is a
great beautifier.

Louisa May Alcott

One word frees us of all the weight and pain of life; that word is love.

Sophocles

Affection is responsible
for nine-tenths of whatever
solid and durable happiness
there is in our lives.

C. S. Lewis

For you see, each day
I love you more,
Today more than
yesterday and less
than tomorrow.

Rosemonde Gérard

Being deeply loved
by someone gives
you strength; loving
someone deeply gives
you courage.

Lao Tzu

Love is everything it's cracked up to be… It really is worth fighting for, being brave for, risking everything for.

Erica Jong

Those who love deeply
never grow old; they may
die of old age, but they
die young.

Dorothy Canfield Fisher

We have the greatest
pre-nuptial agreement
in the world. It's
called love.

Gene Perret

True love stories
never have endings.

Richard Bach

Whatever our souls are
made of, his and mine are
the same.

Emily Brontë, *Wuthering Heights*

Love makes your soul
crawl out from its
hiding place.

Zora Neale Hurston

If I had a single flower for
every time I think about you,
I could walk forever in
my garden.

Claudia Ghandi

Are we not like two
volumes of one book?

Marceline Desbordes-Valmore

I'm so in love, every time I
look at you my soul
gets dizzy.

Jaesse Tyler

He felt now that he was not
simply close to her, but that
he did not know where he
ended and she began.

Leo Tolstoy, *Anna Karenina*

The only true gift is a portion of yourself.

Ralph Waldo Emerson

What a grand thing, to be loved! What a grander thing still, to love!

Victor Hugo

Love is composed of a single soul inhabiting two bodies.

Aristotle

My true love hath my
heart, and I have his.

Philip Sidney

The entire sum of existence
is the magic of being
needed by just one person.

Vi Putnam

Love doesn't make the world go round; love is what makes the ride worthwhile.

Franklin P. Jones

Each morning as I awaken, you're the reason I smile, you're the reason I love.

Jerry Burton

We are each of us angels
with only one wing; and we
can only fly by embracing
one another.

Luciano de Crescenzo

My beloved is mine and I am his.

Bible, Song of Solomon 2:16

Happiness is the meaning and purpose of life, the whole aim and end of human existence.

Aristotle

HAPPILY
EVER
AFTER

I drew my bride,
beneath the moon,
Across my threshold;
happy hour!

Coventry Patmore

Age does not protect you
from love but love to some
extent protects you
from age.

Jeanne Moreau

Let's be a comfortable
couple, and take care of
each other!

Charles Dickens

Grow old along
with me!
The best is yet to be.

Robert Browning

Motto for the bride and
groom: We are a work
in progress with a
lifetime contract.

Phyllis Koss

Our wedding was many years ago. The celebration continues to this day.

Gene Perret

If I know what love is, it is because of you.

Herman Hesse

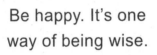

Be happy. It's one
way of being wise.

Colette

ALL YOU NEED IS LOVE

£4.99

ISBN: 978 1 84953 130 6

*'Love is an irresistible desire to be
irresistibly desired.'*

Robert Frost

HEARTFELT WORDS FOR STARRY-EYED LOVERS

When John Lennon wrote that 'all you need is love' back in 1967, perhaps he'd been struck by the lovebug himself. Love is a gift, love is an adventure, love is a many-splendoured thing – love is what makes the world go round, so why not spread a little of the sweet stuff right now?

Here's a book packed with quotations that will have you feeling the love in no time.

IT MUST
BE LOVE

£4.99

ISBN: 978 1 84953 206 8

*'Where love is concerned, too
much is not even enough.'*

Pierre de Beaumarchais

PASSIONATE WORDS
FOR CRAZY LOVERS

You can't eat, you can't sleep, and your heart skips a beat every time a certain someone catches your eye. No, you're not crazy, and you don't need a doctor to tell you the reason for these new sensations – it must be love!

Here's a book packed with dreamy quotations to delight hopeless romantics everywhere.

www.summersdale.com

KEEP CALM FOR BRIDES

KEEP CALM FOR BRIDES

KEEP CALM FOR BRIDES

KEEP CALM FOR BRIDES

KEEP CALM FOR BRIDES

KEEP CALM FOR BRIDES

KEEP CALM FOR BRIDES

KEEP CALM FOR BRIDES

KEEP CALM FOR BRIDES

KEEP CALM FOR BRIDES
KEEP CALM FOR BRIDES
KEEP CALM FOR BRIDES
KEEP CALM FOR BRIDES
KEEP CALM FOR BRIDES
KEEP CALM FOR BRIDES
KEEP CALM FOR BRIDES